THE GNOMES OF GRIMBLEWOOD

DEDICATION

This book is dedicated to my family,
the Adventure Schiras, who help me
make everyday life an adventure.

THE GNOMES OF GRIMBLEWOOD

Enchanting friends to knit, full of magic and mischief

SARAH SCHIRA

SEARCH PRESS

Contents

The Gnomes

Introduction

Once upon a time, there was a knitter who loved gnomes. She was always cold and couldn't understand why she was knitting and knitting (and knitting) gnomes rather than cardigans. All she knew was that, as she stitched on the beard and the gnome popped into itself, complete with a personality and a life history, she would instantly dream of doing it again. But with a red hat. Or a skinny beard. Or a cabled body.

Her family wondered a little bit about all the gnomes accumulating on the shelf. Her teenage son would walk into the room and chuckle, 'Mama's #NeverNotGnoming!' It was an odd pastime, but it filled her with joy.

She published a pattern, calling it 'Never Not Gnoming' (to be in on the joke this time). She expected exactly 12 people to make a gnome with her, and then she would go back to knitting variation after variation by herself. Alone. (Other than the gnomes, of course.)

Except, reader, the story didn't end like that. As this book proves, we can't write 'The End' at the bottom of the page just yet.

At first I thought the gnomes would just come out during the festive season in December, but I hated putting them away. The next year, I told everyone the gnomes were officially 'Snow Gnomes' and they would come out with the first big snowstorm in Autumn, and we wouldn't put them away until the last snow melted in the yard. It gave us a way to welcome the first steely skies hurling snowflakes at us in November, and a joyous 'melt-watch' in April.

It wasn't long, of course, until I bought them a glass cabinet of their very own to sit in, and accepted that I needed gnomes all year round.

What is it about gnomes? Yes, they are speedy, rewarding projects. Yes, they use up left-over yarns. Yes, they make gifts that make people smile. Yes, they let you play with colours. Yes, they are perfect for trying out new knitting skills because they don't need to fit anyone and a wonky gnome just looks more like a gnome. But I think 'The Thing About Gnomes' is two-fold.

First, they are purely for pleasure. In a world that tells us we need to be serious and productive, knitting a gnome says, 'I am playing'. Secondly, there is this magical moment during the assembly process. We're all knitters and we know about knitting. But when you get to assembly, and when you stitch on the nose, pow! The gnome's not just a knitted project anymore, it's a being. That's a moment of creation.

I really want you to play with these patterns; add your ideas and try new things! Gnomes are great to mess around with. To make it extra easy to get started, I've made four of the gnomes interchangeable: because the brim stitch count is the same, you can mix and match the different hat styles with the different body shapes for Gnorri, Gnatalia, Gnolan and Gnarley.

Have fun! Remember, there is no judgment in Grimblewood – any wonkiness is simply gnominess.

Materials

A gnome is made of four ingredients: yarn, fluffy stuffing, weighted stuffing, and not taking yourself too seriously.

Yarns

The gnomes are knitted with a dense gauge/tension, so I recommend using yarns with bounce and stretch since that's easier on our wrists. My favourite yarns for gnomes have a high percentage of wool, as wool loves to be knitted, and knows how to relax and show off your work when blocked.

The gnomes in this book have been knitted in two yarn weights. This is because I wanted you to get excited by the way different colour choices or yarn textures can change a gnome's personality. Plus, not everyone likes working with fine yarn.

I have used the following yarns and yarn weights:

- **fingering (4-ply/weight 1) yarn:**
  Miss Babs Katahdin 437 (100% Superwash Bluefaced Leicester Wool); 100g/437yd/400m; colours used: Blackwatch, Carina, Corset, Gold Rush, Old Gold, Naked.

- **light worsted (DK/8-ply/weight 3) yarn:**
  Rowan Felted Tweed (50% Wool, 25% Alpaca, 25% Viscose); 50g/191yd/175m; colours used: 170 Seafarer, 191 Granite, 193 Cumin, 196 Barn Red, 197 Alabaster, 209 Eden.

For a full list of the yarn quantities for each gnome in this book, and the needles I've used with them, see pages 92 and 93.

If you want to use a different yarn weight than I have, go for it! Experiment and have fun. I recommend you go down two needle sizes from the yarn label and see what the fabric looks like – you want it to have a bit of heft and stiffness to help the gnome stand, and you want it tight enough that the stuffing doesn't show through. Your yardage will be different from what's listed here, so make sure you have extra.

P.S. beards are fabulous for showing off textured yarns. Try bouclé, mohair, or faux fur!

Stuffing

Fluffy stuffing

There are two main options for fluffy stuffing:

- **Polyfill** - this is commercial, plastic-based stuffing found in craft stores. Polyfill is a little better if you need to wash it often, so if you're making a gnome for a child, this might be the way to go.

- **Roving** - this is wool before it's spun. Roving comes in many grades (and price points), and is often available from mills or yarn shops that cater to spinners.

> **NOTE:** you'll need more stuffing than you think!

Weighted stuffing

Since gnomes are tall and narrow, adding weighted stuffing to the base before you close them up shifts their centre of gravity, and helps give them a satisfying heftiness. There are a lot of things you can use for weighted stuffing.

- **Poly pellets** - these little plastic pellets are often found beside polyfill at the craft store, and are ideal for gnomes that might need to be washed.

- **Dried beans, legumes, split peas** - these are great if you live in a drier climate and don't have a pest problem. Choose smaller beans or your gnome could get lumpy.

- **Anything small and convenient** - experiment with aquarium gravel, glass florist's pebbles, pennies, buttons, large metal washers, river rocks, cedar hanger rings.

Whichever you choose, there are two main considerations. First, will your gnome be a toy? If so, remember that kids tend to throw them around or use them to whack each other on the head. Choose something that won't turn your gnome into a weapon, or omit the weighted stuffing entirely.

Second, will this squirm through the knitted fabric? Generally, the gauge/tension of a tightly knit light worsted (DK/8-ply/weight 3) or thinner yarn won't have a problem. A great solution is to put your stuffing into a gauze bag or tie it up in the toe of an old nylon/stocking/pair of tights, before inserting it into your gnome.

Equipment

Notions

You will need standard knitting notions, such as:

- **Scissors or snips** - for cutting yarn.
- **Yarn needle** - for joining different body parts and features, and weaving in yarn.
- **Stitch markers** - removable and regular.
- **Cable needle** - for cable work.

Needles

Gnomes are knitted at a small circumference, so needles that are suitable for small circular knitting will be needed. You can use double-pointed needles (DPNs), the magic loop method, the two-circular-needle method, or flexible DPNs (such as FlexiFlips or CraSyTrio by addi).

For the wider sections of a gnome you can also use short circulars, like the tiny circular needles for socks. However, you'll need a second method for the narrower sections.

Finding the needles that work best for you is key. If you are struggling, don't blame yourself - try a different needle material or knitting method. I advise against using slick needles because they are especially tricky to use when you have only a few stitches on the needle - and having a needle fall out when you're at the tip of a hat is not great for your mood. I like needles made of carbon-fibre because they combine the warm feeling and grip of wood with the stiffness and pointy tips of metal needles.

I've written the patterns to be 'needle agnostic' - they don't assume you're using any one method. I have divided the instructions into sections and you'll use stitch markers to help you note those sections. You can divide the stitches up as works best for you.

The following needle sizes have been used to make all the gnomes in this book:

- 2.25mm (US 1, UK 13)
- 2.5mm (US 1.5, UK 12/13)
- 3.25mm (US 3, UK 10)
- 3.5mm (US 4, UK 9/10)
- 4mm (US 6, UK 8)
- 4.5mm (US 7, UK 7).

Abbreviations

3-3 RC	sl 3 sts to cn and hold in back, k3, k3 from cn
3-2 RC	sl 2 sts to cn and hold in back, k3, k2 from cn
2-2 RC	sl 2 sts to cn and hold in back, k2, k2 from cn
2-1 RC	sl 1 st to cn and hold in back, k2, k1 from cn
1-1 RC	sl 1 st to cn and hold in back, k1, k1 from cn
BOR	beginning of round
cn	cable needle
CO	cast on
dec	decrease
DPNs	double-pointed needles
inc	increase
k	knit
k2tog	knit 2 sts together (1-st decrease)
kfb	knit into the front and back of st (1-st increase)
kfb-M	kfb modified: knit into the front and then place your right needle tip as if to knit into the back of st. Instead of knitting it, slip the loop off the left needle tip (1-st increase)
LT	left twist: knit the 2nd st tbl, then knit the 1st and sl both sts off needle
M	marker
M1L	make 1 left: insert left needle, from front to back, under strand of yarn which runs between next st on left needle and last st on right needle; knit this st tbl (1-st increase)
M1R	make 1 right: insert left needle, from back to front, under strand of yarn which runs between next st on left needle and last st on right needle; knit this st through the front loop (1-st increase)

p	purl
p2tog	purl 2 sts together (1-st decrease)
PM	place marker
RM	remove marker
RS	right side
RT	right twist: k2tog leaving sts on left needle, then knit 1st st again, sl both sts off needle
sl	slip purlwise
SM	slip marker
ssk-M	slip, slip, knit modified: slip the next 2 sts, the 1st one knitwise and the 2nd one purlwise; insert the tip of the left needle, from left to right, into the fronts of those 2 sts and knit them together (1-st decrease)
st(s)	stitch(es)
tbl	through back loop
WS	wrong side
wyib	with yarn in back

Techniques and Tips

Gnomes as toys

Tips for turning your gnomes into toys are scattered throughout the book, but there are three key principles:

- ◅◅◅ **Make sure body parts are securely attached**. Toys are carried by every possible piece. When stitching, stitch from more than one side/direction and make your stitches closer together.

- ◅◅◅ **Toys need denser fluffy stuffing** than decorations to withstand the repeated hugs.

- ◅◅◅ **Don't use weighted stuffing that could cause damage** if the gnome is whacked against a friend's wee noggin - or an adult's bigger noggin! Depending on the size of your weighted stuffing, especially with light worsted (DK/8-ply/weight 3) yarn, put your weighted stuffing in a gauze bag or toe of an old nylon/stocking/pair of tights to keep it inside where it belongs.

Casting on and binding/casting off

Unless noted otherwise, use the long-tail cast-on method to cast on your stitches. Where this cast-on is particularly suited to the piece, I have reminded you to use it in the instructions. To bind/cast off, I use either the regular bind/cast off method or the three-needle bind/cast off method. The latter closes seams securely and invisibly, and means you don't have to graft stitches.

Markers

For all gnome patterns, slip the markers when you reach them.

I-cord

This is a rather miraculous way to knit a tube without trying to work 2-6 stitches in the round.

To work an I-cord: Knit the number of stitches detailed in the pattern. Do not turn work. Slide all stitches to the other end of the needle, switch the needle back to your left hand, bring the yarn around back of work then knit the stitches again. Repeat this round to form an I-cord. After a few rounds, your work will begin to form a tube (see **Fig. A**).

I-cord tips

- ◅◅◅ An I-cord is worked with the right side facing you at all times

- ◅◅◅ If you are working on circular needles, it may be faster to slip the stitches back to the left needle tip rather than slide them along the needle cord

- ◅◅◅ I-cords often look a bit loose on the wrong side, especially when there are 4+ stitches. To prevent this, work the first stitch tightly to minimize the length of yarn coming around the back. Then, after it's done, gently roll the cord between your palms; this will - rather magically - even out the tension.

Fig. A

Picking up stitches from the hat brim

I like to separate the process of picking up stitches from the step where you knit them. With the narrow circumference and tighter gauge/tension, it's so much easier.

1 Fold the hat towards the tip so you're able to work on the outside of the circle rather than trying to get your needles inside the brim. The tip of the hat will be pointing down, with the opening facing towards you.

2 Pick up the stitches all the way around, then join in the body yarn and start knitting with this. The illustrations below show picking up stitches from a ribbed brim (see **Fig. B**) and a rolled brim (see **Fig. C**). See the tips, right, if you need some help on where and how to pick up stitches.

3 Work the body with the hat tip pointing down, and make sure your first stitch from the pick-up is also your first stitch in Round 1. I usually knit with the hat folded back for about one-third of the body to keep it out of the way.

Tips

≪ There's basically no wrong way to pick up stitches. You can pick up a leg of a stitch or the top of a stitch (which I prefer, and is what's shown here).

Essentially, as long as your stitches aren't twisted, and therefore tight and unstretchy, you just need to get approximately the right number of stitches on your needles - in the next round you can increase or decrease a few stitches if necessary. Remember: gnomes are forgiving.

≪ I have added a removable stitch marker to every hat pattern so that you know where to start.

≪ Depending on how comfortable you are with picking up stitches, you might also want to run a contrasting strand of smooth waste yarn through the stitches in the round where I have suggested you add that stitch marker - it makes a nice, bright trail to follow when it's time to pick up.

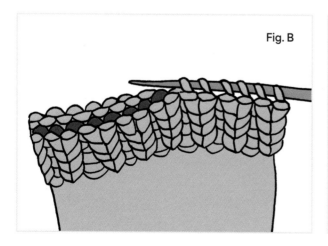

Fig. B

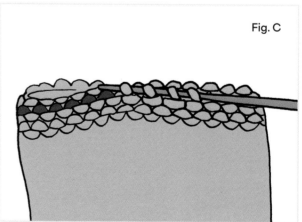

Fig. C

TOP: The brim of Gnoddy's garter-stitch earflap, shown with the sweater ribbing below.

BOTTOM: Detail of Gnicole's ribbed hat brim. The brim remains flipped up and the purl bumps help create a crisper transition from hat to body.

Blocking

Not all gnomes need blocking. Many of the simpler ones are happy just as they are. However, other gnomes need a little water to help them relax and show their best side to the world. In particular, textured patterns, colourwork and cables need help settling in.

There are two main options for blocking gnomes - soaking and steaming.

> NOTE: I'm not talking about the kind of aggressive blocking lace knitting gets; I mean adding a little moisture and letting things relax and be gorgeous.

Soaking

This method mostly means blocking while the gnome is still on the needles (unless you're blocking the hat only, and leaving the body to do its own thing).

1 Block the gnome right before the decreases start at the bottom of the body. You can either plop the whole gnome in a bowl of water, letting the needles dangle over the edge (rather than letting them take a bath as well), or you can thread the gnome on waste yarn for this step.

2 Once the gnome has soaked for 5-15 minutes, gently squeeze the water out as best you can, then roll it in a towel. Gently stand on this gnome-roll, being careful not to snap your needles or puncture your foot.

3 To dry, you can pat the gnome out flat into a position that looks good - not stretched out, just nice and even. If you do this, you will likely get fold lines at the sides. Rotating it several times as it nears dryness is a good option. Or, you can roll up a tea towel (make sure it's smaller than the gnome as you don't want to stretch it out) and insert it up the centre of the gnome body and partways up the hat (see **Fig. D**); this will keep that fold from developing. If you use this method, arrange it so that the gnome does not get flat at the edges (the sides should have a gentle curve rather than a sharp edge) and that the top of the towel does not distort the hat even though the gnome narrows towards the top.

Steaming

Steaming alters your knitting less than a soaking, but it still has a nice effect on the fabric. One of the perks is that you can steam the gnome right at the very end - after it's knitted, stuffed, and assembled. Another perk is that you can use it on multi-coloured gnomes when you're worried about bleeding (I'm looking at you, tragic colourwork gnome incident of 2019).

Use either a clothes iron or a steamer, and hit the gnome with puffs of steam. Rotate the gnome, being careful not to scald your skin! Before you set the gnome to cool and dry, smooth the fabric out and position everything the way you want it to be.

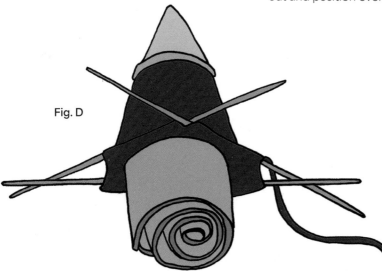

Fig. D

Stuffing

1 Take small amounts of fluffy stuffing then spread them out with your fingers as you place them inside the gnome. Lots of thinner layers are better for filling the space in your gnome, as they don't leave air gaps or create lumps. When I'm working with fluffy stuffing, I envision creating a stack of pancakes rather than dumping in a bunch of apples. As you stuff with one hand from the inside, use the other to check for gaps and help shape from the outside.

2 Add the weighted stuffing. Next, insert a little disc of fluffy stuffing that's larger than the hole you have, tucking it between the knitted fabric and the weighted stuffing. This keeps the pellets from jumping out as you work the final decreases. It also lets you test the balance of your gnome before you work those last decreases: place the gnome on your palm and give it a little shake - does it want to topple right off? If it does, change the ratio of stuffing to include more weighted stuffing.

3 Once it's stuffed, work the final rounds for the gnome. It will be more awkward to knit, so I recommend supporting the weight of the gnome on your lap or on a table in front of you, even putting it in a glass on the table. For tall gnomes, you could try laying it on its side on the table or your lap and then rotating it as you work. Supporting the weight at this stage keeps the final rounds from stretching out.

4 Before knotting the yarn, double-check that you like the look and balance of your stuffing.

> NOTE: if there is a purl ridge on the bottom of the gnome, don't stuff above it - keep the bottom flat.

Fluffy stuffing

Weighted stuffing

Thin pad of fluffy stuffing

Assembly

Knitters are good at knitting, but getting good at assembly might take a bit of practice. Remember, you can pull things out and redo them - just make sure you don't make a knot or clip an end until you like it.

Dealing with ends

Unless otherwise noted, cut ends about 4in (10cm) long.

To knot on a gnome where the wrong side is inaccessible, run the yarn needle under the running thread between two stitches to make a loop. Thread the needle twice through the loop (see **Fig. E**), and then use your thumb and finger to pull the knot as close to the surface of the fabric as possible, while pulling on the yarn with the other hand to tighten. Plunge the yarn through to the other side of the gnome and tug on the end until the knot pops through to the inside of the gnome. Pull the end taut and snip close to the surface - it will vanish inside.

Brim

Part of the charm of the gnomes is the way the brim drapes over the face, hiding the eyes. I also love it when the brim droops over the nose as well. If you want a bigger brim for more droop, add two rounds to the ribbing section for the gnomes that start with a ribbed brim (excluding Gnicole on page 78, whose brim stays flipped up).

Sewing on beards

If the hat has a ribbed brim, flip it up. Sew beard onto the centre-front of the body of the gnome, on the first round of the body, one stitch or so down from top of the beard. Go under a garter-stitch 'ridge' and then over a garter-stitch 'ridge', making sure to catch the body fabric as you go under beard (see **Fig. F**).

Tips

≪≪ **Play with your g-nitting:** Every time you attach a body part or weave in an end, it's an opportunity to tidy something up - use those ends to make your gnome sit straighter or to make them look more rumpled, sew up a hole or hide a 'glitch'.

≪≪ **Position is personality:** How you assemble your gnome will impact its character, so don't rush the process.

≪≪ **Wonkiness is gnominess!:** It's OK if your gnome's features aren't perfectly symmetrical or consistent in size. It marks your gnome's individuality.

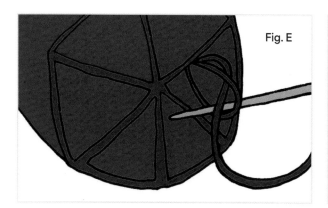

Fig. E

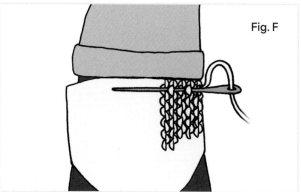

Fig. F

Sewing on arms

Position the arms at the top corners of the beard, on the first round of the body. Attach to the body with whipstitches in a V-shape (see **Fig. G**). If your gnome will be a toy, you'll want to secure the arms more strongly: do more stitches in the V-shape, and then lift the arm and do several stitches underneath, turning the 'V' into a 'Y' (see **Fig. H**). 'Y' do that? Because the odds that the gnome will be carried by the arm are very high!

Feet

Position the feet so that the centre of each foot lines up with an edge of the beard. Use whipstitches to attach the feet to the bottom of the gnome. See also the photograph on page 21. If the gnome has a purled ridge, stitch two rounds in from that ridge. If the gnome does not, experiment with the position so that the feet peep out delightfully and aren't so far back that it forces the gnome to tip over.

Noses

More often than not, I orient my nose stitches vertically to align with the hat and body stitches, but listen to what your gnome whispers to you.

Large nose

With the brim lifted out of the way, if appropriate, sew the nose to the beard with its midpoint centred along the top of the beard. Stitch through the nose (see **Fig. I**) and then through the beard horizontally (see **Fig. J**). Stitch in at least three places, more if it will be a toy. Use your thumb to tilt the nose up and down to give yourself space for the needle. Thread each end of the yarn through from the RS to the WS of the beard. Tie the ends securely together and weave in.

Small nose

With the brim lifted out of the way, if appropriate, sew the nose to the beard with the midpoint centred along the top of the beard. Thread each end of yarn through the beard from the right side to the wrong side. Tie the ends securely together and weave in.

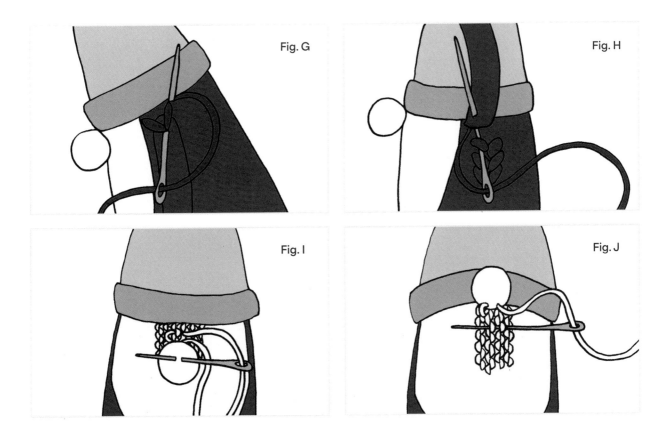

Fig. G

Fig. H

Fig. I

Fig. J

Making Little Features

Arms

Sizes: Small(Medium:Large)

Cast on 4(5:6) sts with the long-tail cast-on method using the needles and hand-colour yarn listed in the pattern. Work I-cord for 1(3:3) rounds (see page 13). Cut hand colour.

Join sleeve colour and work 13(20:25) rounds of I-cord. Cut yarn, leaving a 6in (15cm) tail.

Thread tail onto a yarn needle then take the needle through the sts from right to left to secure. Leave this end for sewing to body later.

Tie the ends from the colour change, thread them onto the yarn needle, and then take the needle up the arm.

Thread the cast-on yarn onto the yarn needle and, again, take the needle up the arm. Pull the ends taut then snip close to the fabric.

To smooth out your gnome's arms, roll each one gently between your palms like a child making a snake from clay.

Small Arms

Medium Arms

Large Arms

Feet

Leaving a 6in (15cm) tail for attaching later, cast on 12 sts using the yarn listed in the pattern and smaller needles. Distribute the sts evenly across the needles, then join for working in the round. Place BOR marker.

Rounds 1–4: k all – 4 rounds.

Round 5: (k1, M1R, k4, M1L, k1) twice – 4-st inc (16 sts).

Round 6: k all.

Round 7: (k1, M1R, k6, M1L, k1) twice – 4-st inc (20 sts).

Rounds 8 and 9: k all – 2 rounds.

Round 10: (k1, ssk-M, k4, k2tog, k1) twice – 4-st dec (16 sts).

Round 11: (k1, ssk-M, k2, k2tog, k1) twice – 4-st dec (12 sts).

Flip the foot inside out, divide the sts evenly across two needles if needed, and then bind/cast off with a 3-needle bind/cast off. Cut yarn. Weave in end from bind/cast off, leaving the cast-on end for later. Turn the foot right-side out. Lightly stuff the ball section of the foot.

Beards

Garter-stitch beard

Both sides of this beard are very similar, but the right side has the edges I prefer. Pick the one you like best.

Leaving a 6in (15cm) tail for attaching later, cast on 12 sts with the long-tail cast-on method, using the needles and yarn listed in pattern.

Row 1 (WS): k all.

Row 2 (RS): k all.

Row 3: k to last st, kfb – 1-st inc (13 sts).

Row 4: k all.

Rows 5-16: repeat Rows 3 and 4 six more times – 12 rows (19 sts).

Rows 17 and 18: k all – 2 rows.

Row 19: k to last 2 sts, k2tog – 1-st dec (18 sts).

Row 20: k all.

Rows 21-32: repeat Rows 19 and 20 six more times – 12 rows (12 sts).

Row 33: k all.

Bind/cast off knitwise.

Cut yarn. Weave in this end.

Block if needed.

Fringe beard

Types: Small and Straight (Wide and Curly)

> TIP: you may find it helpful to note the RS of the fabric with a removable st marker after you work Row 1.

Holding the yarn double throughout, and leaving a 6in (15cm) tail for attaching later, cast on 4(8) sts with the long-tail cast-on method using the needles and yarn listed in pattern.

Row 1 (RS): k2tbl, k to end.

Row 2 (WS): k to last 2 sts, k2tbl.

Repeat Rows 1 and 2 six(eleven) more times.

Do not turn. Use the left needle to pass the second st from the right needle tip over the first st.

Cut yarn. Pull on the loop of the leftmost st until the end pops out. Remove other sts from needle.

Wide & Curly beard: soak and allow to dry.

Both beards: from WS, use the tip of a needle to unravel the columns of live sts (see **Fig. K** then **Fig. L**). To avoid tangles, completely unravel each garter ridge before unravelling the next.

Wide & Curly beard: separate the double strands from each other (the other beard will naturally separate).

Weave in three of the four ends, leaving one of the cast-on ends to attach the beard

NOTE: illustrations show a single strand of yarn for clarity.

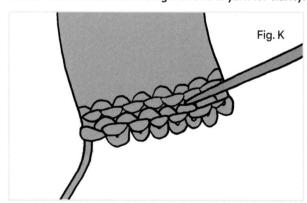

Fig. K

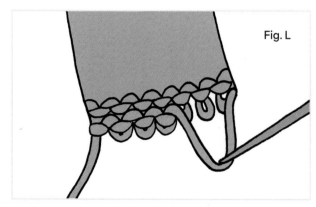

Fig. L

Noses

Small nose

Leaving a 6in (15cm) tail for attaching later, cast on 5 sts with the long-tail cast-on method using the needles and yarn listed in pattern.

Work 5 rounds of I-cord.

Cut yarn, thread the tail onto the yarn needle and then take the needle through the sts from right to left.

To shape the nose, tie together the ends from either side of the I-cord, so that they meet and the I-cord shapes into a little circle (see **Fig. M**). Leave the ends for sewing on.

'Girls with beards?'

I get this question a lot.
My answer is: whyever not?

Large nose

> **NOTE:** I've used both a kfb and kfb-M. The kfb-M is a smoother increase. You can use kfb for every increase if you prefer.

Using yarn and needles listed in pattern, cast on 4 sts. Distribute sts evenly across needles and join for working in the round. Place BOR marker.

Round 1: (kfb) four times – 4-st inc (8 sts).

Round 2: (kfb-M, k1) four times – 4-st inc (12 sts).

Round 3: k all.

Round 4: (kfb-M, k2) four times – 4-st inc (16 sts).

Rounds 5-7: k all – 3 rounds.

Round 8: (k2, k2tog) four times – 4-st dec (12 sts).

Round 9: k all.

Round 10: (k1, k2tog) four times – 4-st dec (8 sts).

Stuff with fluffy stuffing.

Round 11: (k2tog) four times – 4-st dec (4 sts).

Cut yarn, leaving a 6in (15cm) tail. Thread the tail onto the yarn needle then take the needle through the remaining sts. Plunge the needle into the nose through the centre of the final sts and then come out at the side of the sphere. Thread the end from the cast-on onto the yarn needle, take the needle through the middle of the cast-on sts, and come out at the same point where the other end came out (see **Fig. N**).

Pull on the ends to draw the nose into a tidy sphere and then tie ends together. Leave the ends for sewing the nose onto the gnome.

Fig. M

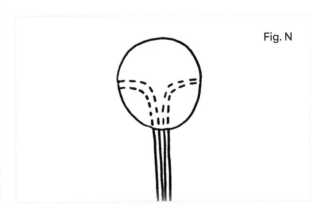

Fig. N

Pockets

Leaving a 6in (15cm) tail for attaching later, cast on 9 sts with the long-tail cast-on method, using the needles and yarn listed in pattern.

Row 1 (RS): k all.

Rows 2, 4, 6 (WS): p to last 2 sts, p2tog – 1-st dec.

Rows 3, 5, 7 (RS): k to last 2 sts, k2tog – 1-st dec.

End after Row 7 (3 sts).

Cut yarn. Thread the tail onto the yarn needle. With RS facing, take the needle through the remaining sts from right to left. Pull tight. Weave in this end. Soak and lay flat to dry.

> **NOTE:** when attaching, don't flatten the top edge across the surface of the fabric. Create a rounded opening to better fit the hand.

Tassels

Cut the cardboard to the desired length of your tassel. Wrap the yarn around the cardboard the number of times indicated in the pattern. Cut the end of the yarn even with the bottom of the cardboard. Insert an 18in (45cm) length of yarn under the wraps at the top of the cardboard and tie the yarn twice. This is the yarn you will use to attach the tassel to the gnome.

Slide cardboard out from the tassel. Wrap a 12in (30cm) length of yarn several times around the strands of your tassel, about one-third from the top. Tie this yarn tightly and hide ends by running them through the wraps and down to the bottom of the tassel. Cut the bottom of the loops. Trim the tassel to tidy up the shape.

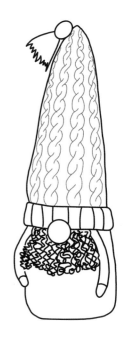

THE GNOMES

Gnoodles
THE SMALLEST GNOME

A visit to the local bookshop changed Gnoodles' life when
a book about Wilson 'Snowflake' Bentley caught her eye.
She was so absorbed that the shop shut up for the night
without her even noticing. She jokingly calls that night her
'metamorphosis'. She ate all the biscuits behind the counter –
apologizing the next morning, of course – and sunrise dawned
with a life's purpose for her. Snowflake photos are tricky
to take, but a snowflake's transient nature excites Gnoodles
and makes her smile when winter clouds glower on
the horizon.

Height

Fingering (4-ply/weight 1):
4½in (11.5cm)

Light worsted (DK/8-ply/weight 3):
6in (15cm)

Gauge/tension

Fingering (4-ply/weight 1):
32 sts and 44 rounds = 4in (10cm) in stockinette/
stocking st in the round on smaller needles

Light worsted (DK/8-ply/weight 3):
24 sts and 36 rounds = 4in (10cm) in stockinette/
stocking st in the round on smaller needles

Yarn

Fingering (4-ply/weight 1):
YARN A: gold (Old Gold)
YARN B: red (Corset)
YARN C: cream (Naked)

Light worsted (DK/8-ply/weight 3):
YARN A: dark navy tweed (170 Seafarer)
YARN B: mid-grey tweed (191 Granite)
YARN C: light grey tweed (197 Alabaster)

Needles

Fingering (4-ply/weight 1):
2.25mm (US 1, UK 13) and 2.5mm (US 1.5, UK 12/13)

Light worsted (DK/8-ply/weight 3):
3.25mm (US 3, UK 10) and 3.5mm (US 4, UK 9/10)

Instructions

HAT

Using yarn A and smaller needles, cast on 28 sts.
Distribute sts evenly across needles then join for
working in the round. Place BOR marker.

Rounds 1–4: (k1, p1) around – 4 rounds.

Place a removable M in WS of the first st of Round 4
to mark the start for picking up body sts.

Rounds 5–10: k all – 6 rounds.

Round 11: (k7, PM) three times, k7.

> **NOTE:** in the rounds that follow, the BOR maker is
> a shaping marker.

Round 12: (k to 2 sts before M, k2tog, SM) four times –
4-st dec (24 sts).

Rounds 13–15: k all – 3 rounds.

Rounds 16–31: repeat Rounds 12–15 four more times –
16 rounds (8 sts).

Round 32: removing M as you go, (k2tog) four times –
4-st dec (4 sts).

Cut yarn. Thread tail onto a yarn needle and take
through sts, pulling them closed. Weave in ends.

ABOVE, FROM LEFT TO RIGHT: fingering (4-ply/weight 1) version;
light worsted (DK/8-ply/weight 3) version; fingering (4-ply/weight 1)
version with teal yarn for the hat.

BODY

Fold the hat brim and about one-third of the hat back. Using smaller needles and working on the WS of the hat, pick up 1 st in every st in the first round above the ribbing, beginning with the st to the left of the removable M (28 sts). Remove M.

Join to work in the round. Join yarn B and then place BOR marker.

Round 1: k all.

Round 2: (kfb, k13) two times - 2-st inc (30 sts).

Rounds 3 and 4: k all - 2 rounds.

Round 5: (k10, PM) two times, k10.

> **NOTE:** in the rounds that follow, BOR marker is a shaping marker.

Round 6: (k1, M1L, k to 1 st before M, M1R, k1, SM) three times - 6-st inc (36 sts).

Rounds 7-10: k all - 4 rounds.

Rounds 11-20: repeat Rounds 6-10 two more times - 10 rounds (48 sts).

Rounds 21-28: k all - 8 rounds.

Weave in end from beginning of body.

Round 29: (k1, k2tog, k to 3 sts before M, ssk-M, k1, SM) three times - 6-st dec (42 sts).

Round 30: k all.

Rounds 31-36: repeat Rounds 29 and 30 three more times, removing M on Round 36 - 6 rounds (24 sts).

Stuff hat and two-thirds of the body with fluffy stuffing.

Round 37: (k1, k2tog) eight times - 8-st dec (16 sts).

> **TIP:** Gnoodles makes a lovely Christmas tree ornament if you leave out the weighted stuffing.

Stuff the body with weighted stuffing. Cover it with a very thin layer of stuffing so the pellets don't jump out as you finish.

Round 38: (k2tog) eight times - 8-st dec (8 sts).

Cut yarn. Thread tail onto a yarn needle and take through remaining sts, pulling them closed. Weave in the ends.

LITTLE FEATURES

Make:

- ⫷⫷⫷ 2 Small Arms (see page 20), using larger needles and yarns B and C.
- ⫷⫷⫷ 1 Small & Straight Fringe Beard (see page 22), using larger needles and yarn C.
- ⫷⫷⫷ 1 Small Nose (see page 23), using larger needles and yarn C.

MAKING UP

Fold brim up. Sew beard onto first round of body. Centre and sew nose on top of beard. Sew arms onto first round of body at corners of the beard. Fold the brim down.

OPPOSITE: light worsted (DK/8-ply/weight 3) version.

ABOVE, FROM LEFT TO RIGHT: light worsted (DK/8-ply/weight 3) version;
fingering (4-ply/weight 1) version.

Gnoddy
THE EARFLAP GNOME

Gnoddy has a gnose for adventure. She likes to walk
to the café for a cup of acorn and chanterelle tea,
and then sets off in a random direction. She smiles at
everyone she passes and makes friends easily. If you see
her walking one morning, be sure to chat with her –
you never know where her friendship will take you.

Height

Fingering (4-ply/weight 1):
5½in (14cm)

Light worsted (DK/8-ply/weight 3):
7¼in (18.5cm)

Gauge/tension

Fingering (4-ply/weight 1):
32 sts and 44 rounds = 4in (10cm) in stockinette/
stocking st in the round on smaller needles

Light worsted (DK/8-ply/weight 3):
24 sts and 36 rounds = 4in (10cm) in stockinette/
stocking st in the round on smaller needles

Yarn

Fingering (4-ply/weight 1):
YARN A: gold (Old Gold)
YARN B: variegated light gold (Gold Rush)
YARN C: cream (Naked)
YARN D: teal (Blackwatch)

Light worsted (DK/8-ply/weight 3):
YARN A: red tweed (196 Barn Red)
YARN B: dark navy tweed (170 Seafarer)
YARN C: light grey tweed (197 Alabaster)
YARN D: mustard tweed (193 Cumin)

Needles

Fingering (4-ply/weight 1):
2.25mm (US 1, UK 13) and 2.5mm (US 1.5, UK 12/13)

Light worsted (DK/8-ply/weight 3):
3.25mm (US 3, UK 10) and 3.5mm (US 4, UK 9/10)

Instructions

> **NOTE:** we begin by making two earflaps, which are knitted flat. After they're made, use the knitted cast-on method to add sts then join to work in the round.

HAT

Using yarn A and smaller needles, cast on 3 sts.

Rows 1 and 2: k all – 2 rows.

Rows 3 and 4: kfb, k across – 2 rows (5 sts).

Rows 5-10: k all – 6 rows.

Cut yarn and set this earflap aside, either on a spare needle or on waste yarn.

Make another earflap, but don't cut the yarn.

Hold needle with the second earflap in your left hand and use the knitted cast-on to cast on 18 sts. Turn this needle and hold it in your right hand.

If needed, place first earflap back on needle. Hold needle with first earflap in your left hand so that the st with the yarn tail is closest to the right tip. Knit across this earflap using the right needle and the working yarn.

Turn work again. Use the knitted cast-on to cast on 8 sts.

You will now have 36 sts on the needle: 5 sts earflap, 18 sts back, 5 sts earflap, and 8 sts front. Distribute sts evenly across needles and join for working in the round. Place BOR marker.

Round 1: p all.

Round 2: k all.

Rounds 3 and 4: repeat Rounds 1 and 2 – 2 rounds.

Round 5: p all.

Cut yarn. Add a removable M on the WS of the 14th st of Round 5 to mark centre-back st for body pick-up.

Join yarn B.

Rounds 6-16: k all – 11 rounds.

Round 17: (k6, PM) six times.

> **NOTE:** in the rounds that follow, the BOR marker is a shaping marker.

Decrease Round: (k to 2 sts before M, k2tog, SM) six times – 6-st dec.

Round 19: k all.

Repeat Decrease Round and Round 19 until each section has 3 sts (18 sts in total), then repeat Decrease Round every round until 6 sts in total remain.

Cut yarn. Thread tail onto a yarn needle and take through remaining sts, pulling them closed.

NOTE: picking up body sts is easier if you don't weave in ends until later.

Pattern notes

Gnoddy's sweater (see page 38) is knitted right onto the hat!

After picking up sts inside the hat, you'll work a little raglan sweater before picking up sts for her body from the sweater hem.

HANDS/BOBBLE

> NOTE: make 1 with yarn A (bobble) and 2 with yarn C (hands).

Using larger needles, cast on 6 sts.

Work 8 rounds of I-cord.

Cut yarn. Thread tail onto a yarn needle and take through the sts from right to left. To shape, tie ends from either side so the tips meet and the I-cord shapes into a little circle (see **Fig. M** on page 23). Thread one end onto a yarn needle and use whipstitch to join I-cord ends to each other. Leave ends for attaching later.

Attach yarn A bobble to the top of the hat. Set aside the two in yarn C for now.

BODY/SWEATER

Fold the brim and about one-third of the hat back. Using smaller needles and working on the WS of the hat, pick up 1 st in every st in Round 5 of the hat, beginning with the st to the left of the removable M (36 sts).

Distribute sts evenly across needles then join to work in the round. Join yarn D. Place BOR marker.

Round 1: k all.

Rounds 2-6: (k1, p1) around – 5 rounds.

Round 7: (k6, PM) two times, k12, (PM, k6) two times.

> NOTE: in the rounds that follow, BOR marker is NOT a shaping marker.

Round 8: (k to 1 st before M, kfb, SM, kfb) four times, k to end of round – 8-st inc (44 sts).

Round 9: k all.

Rounds 10-13: repeat Rounds 8 and 9 two more times – 4 rounds (60 sts).

Round 14: k to M, remove M, place next 12 sts on waste yarn, remove M, turn work and cast on 4 sts over the underarm gap using the knitted cast-on, turn work and k to next M, remove M, place next 12 sts on waste yarn, remove M, turn work and cast on 4 sts over the gap using the knitted cast-on, turn work and k to end (44 sts).

Rounds 15 and 16: k all – 2 rounds.

Round 17: (k11, M1L) four times – 4-st inc (48 sts).

Rounds 18-22: k all – 5 rounds.

Round 23: (k12, M1L) four times – 4-st inc (52 sts).

Rounds 24-28: k all – 5 rounds.

Place removable M in first st of Round 28 on WS to mark the start for picking up body sts.

Rounds 29 and 30: (k1, p1) around – 2 rounds.

Bind/cast off in pattern. Weave in ends.

Sleeves

Place sts from one sleeve onto needles and distribute evenly across needles for working in the round.

Round 1: using yarn D, k12, pick up and k 2 sts in gap, PM for BOR, pick up and k 2 sts (16 sts).

Round 2: k all.

Round 3: k2tog, k to last 2 sts, ssk-M – 2-st dec (14 sts).

Rounds 4-7: repeat Rounds 2 and 3 two more times – 4 rounds (10 sts).

Rounds 8-11: k all – 4 rounds.

Rounds 12 and 13: (k1, p1) around – 2 rounds.

Bind/cast off in pattern. Cut yarn, leaving a 6in (15cm) tail. Weave in the ends in the armpit, closing any holes. Leave the cuff end open to allow easier hand insertion.

Repeat with second sleeve.

Attach hands

Thread both ends from a hand onto the yarn needle and insert it down the sleeve to lodge the hand into the cuff. Pinching the ends and sleeve together in one hand can keep the hand in place and make securing it easier. Using the end of yarn D from the cuff, secure the hand by piercing through the cuff and hand, coming out the other side. Work around the cuff so that you have gone through the hand at least four times in an asterisk-style pattern. Weave in the cuff end. Hand ends can remain loose in sleeve/body.

Light worsted (DK/8-ply/ weight 3) version – left; fingering (4-ply/weight 1) version – middle. The light worsted (DK/8-ply/ weight 3) version on the far right features a three-colour sweater worked in two-round stripes. Two extra rounds were added before the ribbing to complete the stripe sequence. The arms were then sewn to the body after it was stuffed.

LOWER BODY

Fold the hem and about one-third of the sweater back. Using smaller needles and working on the WS of the sweater, pick up 1 st in every st of the first round above the ribbing, beginning with the st to the left of the removable M (52 sts). Remove M. Work with hem folded away and hat facing down.

Distribute sts evenly across needles then join to work in the round. Join yarn A. Place BOR marker.

Rounds 1–12: k all – 12 rounds.

Round 13: p all.

Round 14: k all.

Round 15: (k11, k2tog) four times – 4-st dec (48 sts).

Weave in the end from the lower body pick-up.

Stuff arms.

> **TIP:** use the eraser end of a pencil to make stuffing the arms easier.

Round 16: (k6, k2tog, PM) six times – 6-st dec (42 sts).

Decrease Round: (k to 2 sts before M, k2tog) around – 6 sts dec.

Repeat Decrease Round until each section has 5 sts (30 sts in total).

Stuff hat and the body to the bottom of the sweater hem with fluffy stuffing.

Repeat Decrease Round until each section has 3 sts (18 sts in total).

Stuff the body with weighted stuffing up to the garter ridge. Cover it with a very thin layer of stuffing so the pellets don't jump out as you finish.

Repeat Decrease Round until only 6 sts remain, removing M.

Cut yarn. Thread tail onto yarn needle and take through remaining sts, pulling them closed. Weave in the end.

LITTLE FEATURES

Make:

- 1 Small & Straight Fringe Beard (see page 22) using larger needles and yarn C.
- 1 Large Nose (see page 23) using larger needles and yarn C.

MAKING UP

Fold brim up. Sew beard onto first round of sweater. Centre and sew nose on top of beard. Fold brim down. Sit back and be charmed by your gnew friend.

OPPOSITE, FROM LEFT TO RIGHT:
fingering (4-ply/weight 1) version;
light worsted (DK/8-ply/weight 3) version.

Gnarley
THE WAVY GNOME

Gnarley is an avid mountain biker. Grimblewood has
a lot of gnarly paths that get the adrenaline flowing.
He likes to recover with a plate of scones and nut butter
before washing his bike. 'Tummy first, gears second,'
is his post-ride motto.

Height

Fingering (4-ply/weight 1):
7in (18cm)

Light worsted (DK/8-ply/weight 3):
9in (23cm)

Gauge/tension

Fingering (4-ply/weight 1):
32 sts and 44 rounds = 4in (10cm) in stockinette/
stocking st in the round on smaller needles

Light worsted (DK/8-ply/weight 3):
24 sts and 36 rounds = 4in (10cm) in stockinette/
stocking st in the round on smaller needles

Yarn

Fingering (4-ply/weight 1):
YARN A: gold (Old Gold)
YARN B: cream (Naked)

Light worsted (DK/8-ply/weight 3):
YARN A: red tweed (196 Barn Red)
YARN B: light grey tweed (197 Alabaster)

Needles

Fingering (4-ply/weight 1):
2.25mm (US 1, UK 13) and 2.5mm (US 1.5, UK 12/13)

Light worsted (DK/8-ply/weight 3):
3.25mm (US 3, UK 10) and 3.5mm (US 4, UK 9/10)

Instructions

HAT

Using yarn A and smaller needles, cast on 48 sts. Distribute sts evenly across needles and join for working in the round. Place BOR marker.

Rounds 1-4: (p3, k3) around – 4 rounds.

Place removable M in first st of Round 4 on WS to mark the start for picking up body sts.

Rounds 5-30: k all – 26 rounds.

If needed, rearrange sts equally on 2 needles. Hold needles parallel and with yarn coming off the back needle.

Bind/cast off with WS together with a 3-needle bind/cast off. Weave in ends.

BODY

> NOTE: don't be alarmed by the pattern length coming up
> – we are subtly shaping the body and spacing the
> increases. Nothing changes in the wave columns,
> only in the stockinette/stocking sts between them.

Fold the brim and about one-third of the hat back. Using smaller needles and working on the WS of the hat, pick up 1 st in every st in the first round above the ribbing, beginning with the st to the left of the removable M (48 sts). Remove M.

Join to work in the round. Join yarn A and place BOR marker.

Rounds 1 and 2: k all – 2 rounds.

> NOTE: for Rounds 3-49 either follow Charts 1-4 or the
> Written Instructions (see pages 45-48). Chart 1
> applies to Rounds 3-13, Chart 2 applies to Rounds
> 14-25, Chart 3 applies to Rounds 26-37, and Chart 4
> applies to Rounds 38-49.

ABOVE: light worsted (DK/8-ply/weight 3) version.

Written Instructions for Chart 1
Round 3: (k4, p2) eight times.
Round 4: (k3, LT, k1) eight times.
Round 5: (k3, p1, k1, p1) eight times.
Round 6: (k4, LT) eight times.
Round 7: (k3, p2, k1) eight times.
Round 8: k all.
Round 9: (k3, p2, k1) eight times.
Round 10: (k4, RT) eight times.
Round 11: (k3, p1, k1, p1) eight times.
Round 12: (k3, RT, k1) eight times.
Round 13: (k4, p2) eight times.

KEY:

☐	k
•	p
╳	LT
╳	RT

CHART 1

Repeat Chart 1 eight times per round.

CHART 2

Repeat Chart 2 four times per round.

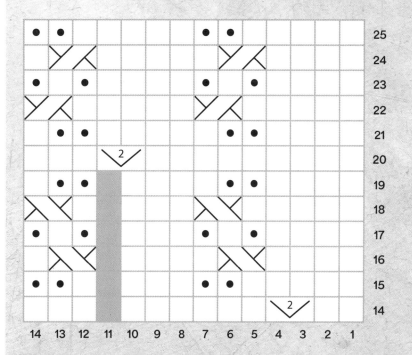

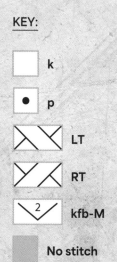

KEY:

☐	k
•	p
LT symbol	LT
RT symbol	RT
kfb-M symbol 2	kfb-M
▨	No stitch

Written Instructions for Chart 2

Round 14: (k2, kfb-M, k9) four times – 4-st inc (52 sts).

Round 15: (k5, p2, k4, p2) four times.

Round 16: ((k4, LT) two times, k1) four times.

Round 17: (k4, p1, k1, p1, k3, p1, k1, p1) four times.

Round 18: (k5, LT, k4, LT) four times.

Round 19: ((k4, p2) two times, k1) four times.

Round 20: (k9, kfb-M, k3) four times – 4-st inc (56 sts).

Round 21: (k4, p2, k5, p2, k1) four times.

Round 22: (k5, RT) eight times.

Round 23: (k4, p1, k1, p1) eight times.

Round 24: (k4, RT, k5, RT, k1) four times.

Round 25: (k5, p2) eight times.

CHART 3

Repeat Chart 3 four times per round.

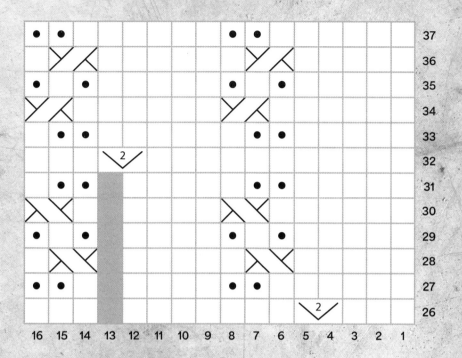

Written Instructions for Chart 3

Round 26: (k3, kfb-M, k10) four times – 4-st inc (60 sts).
Round 27: (k6, p2, k5, p2) four times.
Round 28: ((k5, LT) two times, k1) four times.
Round 29: (k5, p1, k1, p1, k4, p1, k1, p1) four times.
Round 30: (k6, LT, k5, LT) four times.
Round 31: ((k5, p2) two times, k1) four times.
Round 32: (k11, kfb-M, k3) four times – 4-st inc (64 sts).
Round 33: (k5, p2, k6, p2, k1) four times.
Round 34: (k6, RT) eight times.
Round 35: (k5, p1, k1, p1) eight times.
Round 36: (k5, RT, k6, RT, k1) four times.
Round 37: (k6, p2) eight times.

CHART 4

Repeat Chart 4 four times per round.

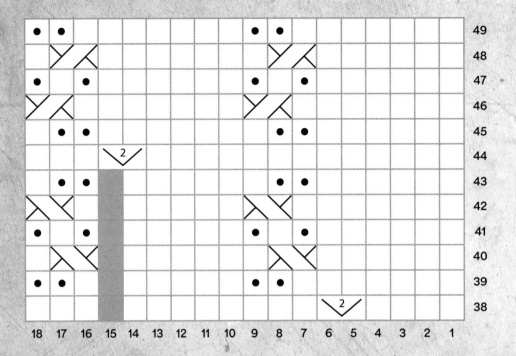

KEY:

☐	k
●	p
⧅	LT
⧄	RT
⌄2	kfb-M
▨	No stitch

Written Instructions for Chart 4

Round 38: (k4, kfb-M, k11) four times – 4-st inc (68 sts).

Round 39: (k7, p2, k6, p2) four times.

Round 40: ((k6, LT) two times, k1) four times.

Round 41: (k6, p1, k1, p1, k5, p1, k1, p1) four times.

Round 42: (k7, LT, k6, LT) four times.

Round 43: ((k6, p2) two times, k1) four times.

Round 44: (k13, kfb-M, k3) four times – 4-st inc (72 sts).

Round 45: (k6, p2, k7, p2, k1) four times.

Round 46: (k7, RT) eight times.

Round 47: (k6, p1, k1, p1) eight times.

Round 48: (k6, RT, k7, RT, k1) four times.

Round 49: (k7, p2) eight times.

Weave in the end from the beginning of the body.

Round 50: k all.

Round 51: p all.

Round 52: (k12, PM) six times.

> NOTE: in the rounds that follow, the BOR maker is a shaping marker.

Decrease Round: (k to 2 sts before M, k2tog, SM) six times – 6-st dec.

Repeat Decrease Round until each section has 6 sts (36 sts total).

Stuff hat and two-thirds of the body with fluffy stuffing.

Repeat Decrease Round until each section has 4 sts (24 sts total).

Stuff the body with weighted stuffing up to the garter ridge. Cover it with a very thin layer of stuffing so the pellets don't jump out as you finish.

Repeat Decrease Round until only 6 sts remain, removing M.

Cut yarn. Thread tail onto yarn needle and take through remaining sts, pulling them closed.

Weave in end.

LITTLE FEATURES

Make:

- ⫷ 1 Garter-stitch Beard (see page 22) using larger needles and yarn B.
- ⫷ 1 Large Nose (see page 23) using larger needles and yarn B.

MAKING UP

Fold brim up. Sew beard onto first round of body. Centre and sew nose on top of beard. Fold brim down. Now, go have a plate of scones together.

ABOVE, FROM LEFT TO RIGHT:
fingering (4-ply/weight 1) version;
light worsted (DK/8-ply/weight 3) version.

49

On the day of the first snow, an impromptu holiday is always called across Grimblewood. Exploring vistas remade, picnicking by a fire, and singing songs to the new drifts... Gnomes know what's most important.

Gnatalia
THE COLOURWORK GNOME

Gnatalia works as a garment historian for the Ladybug Queen. She is secretly working on a new beard apron to protect gnomes' most striking feature. She was inspired by a blacksmith's leather Bearde-Pocket from the 7th century G.C.E. that once shielded a beard from sparks.

Height

Fingering (4-ply/weight 1):
7½in (19cm)

Light worsted (DK/8-ply/weight 3):
9½in (24cm)

Gauge/tension

Fingering (4-ply/weight 1):
32 sts and 44 rounds = 4in (10cm) in stockinette/ stocking st in the round on smaller needles

Light worsted (DK/8-ply/weight 3):
24 sts and 36 rounds = 4in (10cm) in stockinette/ stocking st in the round on smaller needles

Yarn

Fingering (4-ply/weight 1):
YARN A: teal (Blackwatch)
YARN B: red (Corset)
YARN C: cream (Naked)
YARN D: gold (Old Gold)
YARN E: slate grey (Carina)

Light worsted (DK/8-ply/weight 3):
YARN A: red tweed (196 Barn Red)
YARN B: dark navy tweed (170 Seafarer)
YARN C: light grey tweed (197 Alabaster)
YARN D: mint green tweed (209 Eden)
YARN E: mustard tweed (193 Cumin)

Needles

Fingering (4-ply/weight 1):
2.25mm (US 1, UK 13) and 2.5mm (US 1.5, UK 12/13)

Light worsted (DK/8-ply/weight 3):
3.25mm (US 3, UK 10) and 3.5mm (US 4, UK 9/10)

Instructions

HAT

> **NOTE 1:** you will place removable st markers to help you fold the hat – place one in the twelfth st of Round 21 and place one in the last st of Round 60.
>
> **NOTE 2:** the charts on page 56 feature the colours for the fingering (4-ply/weight 1) gnome. If you are making the light worsted (DK/8-ply/weight 3) gnome, in Chart 1 simply swap yarn A for yarn A listed under the light worsted weight gnome opposite, yarn B for yarn B, and so on. For Chart 2, use yarn B for Rounds 70 and 71, yarn A for Round 72, and yarn D for Rounds 73 and 74.

Using yarn A and smaller needles, cast on 48 sts. Distribute sts evenly across needles and join for working in the round. Place BOR marker.

Rounds 1-4: (k1, p1) around – 4 rounds.

Cut yarn A. Place removable M in first st of round 4 on WS to mark the start for picking up body sts.

Rounds 5-24: work Chart 1 or follow Written Instructions on page 56 eight times per round.

Cut all yarns except yarn C. Use yarn C until instructed otherwise.

Round 25: k all.

Round 26: (k8, PM) six times.

> **NOTE:** in the rounds that follow, BOR marker is NOT a shaping marker.

Round 27: (k to 2 sts before M, k2tog, SM) six times – 6-st dec (42 sts).

Rounds 28-36: k all – 9 rounds.

Rounds 37-66: repeat Rounds 27-36 three more times, placing a removable M in last st of Round 60 – 30 rounds (24 sts).

Round 67: (k to 2 sts before M, k2tog, SM) six times – 6-st dec (18 sts).

Rounds 68-76: work Chart 2 or follow Written Instructions on page 56 nine times per round.

Cut all yarns except yarn C and use yarn C to finish hat.

Rounds 77-86: repeat Rounds 27-36 one more time – 10 rounds (12 sts).

Round 87: removing M as you go, (k2tog) six times – 6-st dec (6 sts).

Rounds 88-92: k all – 5 rounds.

Round 93: (k2tog) three times – 3-st dec (3 sts).

Cut yarn. Thread tail onto a yarn needle and take through the live stitches on the needle from right to left. Weave in ends. Block.

OPPOSITE: fingering (4-ply/weight 1) version.
LEFT: light worsted (DK/8-ply/weight 3) version.

CHART 1

Repeat Chart 1 eight times per round.

† Remember to place a removable st marker in the 12th st of Round 21.

KEY:

- ■ Yarn A
- ■ Yarn B
- □ Yarn C
- ▨ Yarn D

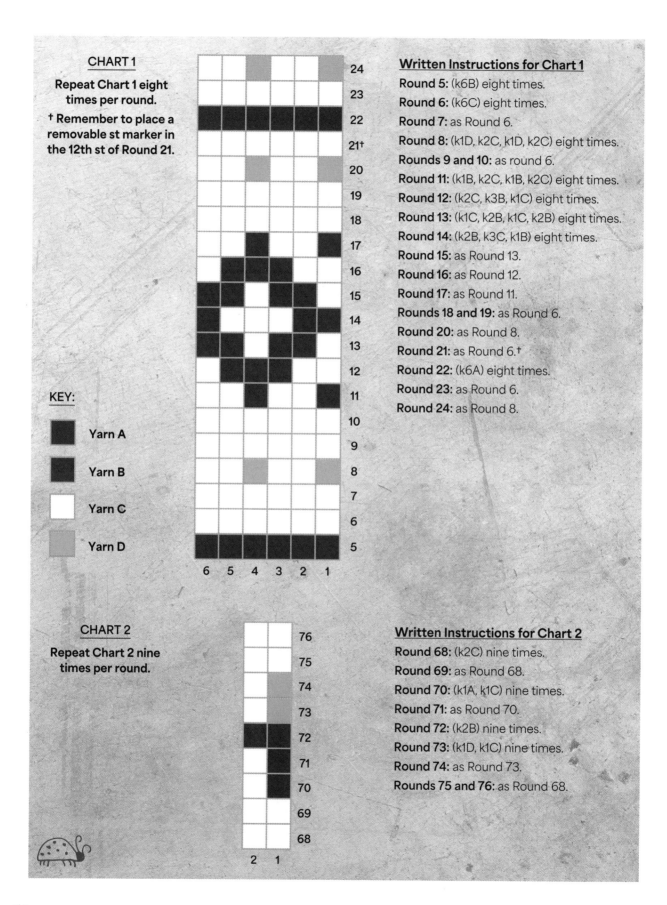

Written Instructions for Chart 1

Round 5: (k6B) eight times.

Round 6: (k6C) eight times.

Round 7: as Round 6.

Round 8: (k1D, k2C, k1D, k2C) eight times.

Rounds 9 and 10: as round 6.

Round 11: (k1B, k2C, k1B, k2C) eight times.

Round 12: (k2C, k3B, k1C) eight times.

Round 13: (k1C, k2B, k1C, k2B) eight times.

Round 14: (k2B, k3C, k1B) eight times.

Round 15: as Round 13.

Round 16: as Round 12.

Round 17: as Round 11.

Rounds 18 and 19: as Round 6.

Round 20: as Round 8.

Round 21: as Round 6.†

Round 22: (k6A) eight times.

Round 23: as Round 6.

Round 24: as Round 8.

CHART 2

Repeat Chart 2 nine times per round.

Written Instructions for Chart 2

Round 68: (k2C) nine times.

Round 69: as Round 68.

Round 70: (k1A, k1C) nine times.

Round 71: as Round 70.

Round 72: (k2B) nine times.

Round 73: (k1D, k1C) nine times.

Round 74: as Round 73.

Rounds 75 and 76: as Round 68.

BODY

Fold the brim and about one-third of the hat back. Using smaller needles and working on the WS of the hat, pick up 1 st in every st in the last round of yarn A, beginning with the st to the left of the removable M (48 sts). Remove marker.

Join to work in the round, then join in yarn E. Place a BOR marker.

Rounds 1 and 2: k all – 2 rounds.

Round 3: k6, (PM, k12) three times, PM, k6.

> NOTE: in the rounds that follow, BOR marker is NOT a shaping marker.

Round 4: (k to 1 st before M, M1R, k1, SM, k1, M1L) four times, k to end – 8-st inc (56 sts).

Round 5: k all.

Round 6: (k to 1 st before M, M1R, k1, SM, k1, M1L) four times, k to end – 8-st inc (64 sts).

Rounds 7 and 8: k all – 2 rounds.

Rounds 9-20: repeat Rounds 6-8 four more times – 12 rounds (96 sts).

Rounds 21-34: k all – 14 rounds.

Round 35: (k to 3 sts before M, ssk-M, k1, SM, k1, k2tog) four times, k to end – 8-st dec (88 sts).

Round 36: k all.

Rounds 37-42: repeat Rounds 35 and 36 three more times – 6 rounds (64 sts).

Cut 18in (45cm) of yarn C and thread onto yarn needle. Fold the hat so that the removable M placed in Rounds 21 and 60 meet. A triangle shape will have formed, with two corners on top of the hat and one on the side where it meets the removable M.

Sew the hat layers together at the three corners of the triangle created.

Weave in the ends of yarn C and the end from the beginning of the body. Remove M from hat.

Return to working on the body.

Round 43: removing M as you go, (k2, k2tog) sixteen times – 16-st dec (48 sts).

Rounds 44 and 45: k all – 2 rounds.

If you intend to make Gnatalia into a toy, see the pattern note, below left. Lightly stuff hat up to the fold line with fluffy stuffing. The hat will be flatter at the top and more round towards the brim as you move away from the fold. Firmly stuff two-thirds of the body with fluffy stuffing.

Round 46: (k1, k2tog) sixteen times – 16-st dec (32 sts).

Rounds 47 and 48: k all – 2 rounds.

Round 49: (k2tog) sixteen times – 16-st dec (16 sts).

Fill with weighted stuffing. Cover with a very thin layer of stuffing so the pellets don't jump out as you finish.

Round 50: (k2tog) eight times – 8-st dec (8 sts).

Cut yarn. Thread tail onto a yarn needle and take through remaining sts, pulling them closed. Weave in the end.

Pattern note

If your Gnatalia will be a toy, I recommend either sewing along the entire top fold so that the stuffing stays below the fold, or not folding the hat and stuffing all the way to the tip. (See instructions after Rounds 44 and 45.)

LITTLE FEATURES

Make:

- 2 Medium Arms (see page 20) using larger needles and yarns C and E.

- 1 Garter-stitch Beard (see page 22) using larger needles and yarn C.

- 1 Large Nose (see page 23) using larger needles and yarn C.

- 1 Tassel (see page 25) with yarns A, B, and D together and wrapping six times. Finished height of tassel: 1½in (4cm) for the fingering (4-ply/weight 1) version or 2½in (6.5cm) for the light worsted (DK/8-ply/weight 3) version.

MAKING UP

Fold brim up. Sew beard onto first round of body. Centre and sew nose on top of beard. Sew arms onto first round of body at the corners of the beard. Fold brim down. Sew tassel to tip of hat. Flick the tassel with your finger and smile.

Gnomes enjoy a good boulder. Why? Well, there's no mischief in a boulder, and they also make excellent places to perch. Gnomes do so love to appreciate a good view.

Gnorri
THE POCKET-BEARD GNOME

Once a gardener for the Ancient Oak, Gnorri is now enjoying
a new chapter of life on the Woodland Council. It's more
bylaws and fewer arcane potions than he had hoped,
but he's making the best of it. And he did get that great tip
on gathering pansy petals at twilight that changed how his
gourd growth potion works.

Height

Fingering (4-ply/weight 1):
8in (20cm)

Light worsted (DK/8-ply/weight 3):
10½in (26.5cm)

Gauge/tension

Fingering (4-ply/weight 1):
32 sts and 44 rounds = 4in (10cm) in stockinette/
stocking st in the round on smaller needles

Light worsted (DK/8-ply/weight 3):
24 sts and 36 rounds = 4in (10cm) in stockinette/
stocking st in the round on smaller needles

Yarn

Fingering (4-ply/weight 1):
YARN A: red (Corset)
YARN B: slate grey (Carina)
YARN C: cream (Naked)

Light worsted (DK/8-ply/weight 3):
YARN A: mint green tweed (209 Eden)
YARN B: red tweed (196 Barn Red)
YARN C: light grey tweed (197 Alabaster)

Needles

Fingering (4-ply/weight 1):
2.25mm (US 1, UK 13) and 2.5mm (US 1.5, UK 12/13)

Light worsted (DK/8-ply/weight 3):
3.25mm (US 3, UK 10) and 3.5mm (US 4, UK 9/10)

Instructions

HAT

Using yarn A and smaller needles, cast on 48 sts.
Distribute sts evenly across needles and join for
working in the round. Place BOR marker.

Rounds 1-4: (k1, p1) around – 4 rounds.

Place removable M in first st of Round 4 on WS to mark
the start for picking up body sts.

Rounds 5-11: k all – 7 rounds.

Round 12: (k12, PM) three times, k12.

> **NOTE:** in the rounds that follow, BOR marker is
> a shaping marker.

Round 13: (k to 2 sts before M, k2tog, SM) four times –
4-st dec (44 sts).

Rounds 14-17: k all – 4 rounds.

Rounds 18-62: repeat Rounds 13-17 nine more times –
45 rounds (8 sts).

Round 63: removing M as you go, (k2tog) four times –
4-st dec (4 sts).

Cut yarn. Thread tail onto a yarn needle and take
through sts, pulling them closed. Weave in ends.

BODY

Fold the brim and about one-third of the hat back. Using smaller needles and working on the WS of the hat, pick up 1 st in every st in the first round above the ribbing, beginning with the st to the left of the removable M (48 sts). Remove M.

Join to work in the round. Join yarn B and place a BOR marker.

Rounds 1-5: k all – 5 rounds.

Round 6: (k16, PM) two times, k16.

> NOTE: in the rounds that follow, BOR marker is a shaping marker.

Round 7: (k2, M1L, k to 2 sts before M, M1R, k2, SM) three times – 6-st inc (54 sts).

Rounds 8-16: k all – 9 rounds.

Rounds 17-36: repeat Rounds 7-16 two more times – 20 rounds (66 sts).

Weave in the end from the beginning of the body.

Round 37: p all.

Round 38: k11, PM, (k11, SM, k11, PM) twice, k11 – 6 markers now in place.

Decrease Round: (k to 2 sts before M, k2tog, SM) six times – 6-st dec.

Repeat Decrease Round until each section has 6 sts (36 sts total).

Stuff hat and two-thirds of the body with fluffy stuffing.

Repeat Decrease Round until each section has 4 sts (24 sts total).

Stuff the body with weighted stuffing up to the garter ridge. Cover with a very thin layer of stuffing so the pellets don't jump out as you finish.

Repeat Decrease Round until only 6 sts remain, removing M.

Cut yarn. Thread tail onto a yarn needle and take through remaining sts, pulling them closed. Weave in the end.

LITTLE FEATURES

Make:

- 2 Medium Arms (see page 20) using larger needles and yarns C and B.
- 1 Garter-stitch Beard (see page 22) using larger needles and yarn C.
- 1 Large Nose (see page 23) using larger needles and yarn C.
- 2 Pockets (see page 24) using larger needles and yarn A.
- 2 Feet (see page 21) using larger needles and yarn B.

MAKING UP

Sew pockets onto beard as shown: match the height of the outer corner with the corner of the beard and tilt inner corner of the pocket diagonally, 3 sts higher.

Fold brim up. Sew beard onto first round of body. Centre and sew nose on top of beard. Sew arms onto first round of body at the corners of the beard. Fold the brim down.

Sew feet to bottom of body on the second round inside the purl ridge using whipstitch, positioning them centred at the edges of the beard.

What does one keep in a pocket? It's a matter of personal choice, of course, but with pockets sweeping the forest of Grimblewood, some gnomes have formed a Pocket Club.

Which toadstools keep well? How do you keep a pocket organized? Should the pocket colour be seasonal?

They also debate the merits of one pocket (dashing! fashionable!) versus two (economical! more storage!).

ABOVE, FROM LEFT TO RIGHT: variation on the light worsted (DK/8-ply/weight 3) gnome with a four-round stripe; fingering (4-ply/weight 1) version; variation on Gnoodles the Smallest Gnome (page 28) with a four-round stripy hat, fringe beard and pocket; light worsted (DK/8-ply/weight 3) version.

Gnolan
THE SWIRLY GNOME

Gnolan performs volunteer magic shows at the hospital on the weekends. At first, they expected he'd only perform in the children's ward, but he convinced them that everyone needs a little magic and a lot of smiles.

Height

Fingering (4-ply/weight 1):
10in (25.5cm)

Light worsted (DK/8-ply/weight 3):
13½in (34.5cm)

Gauge/tension

Fingering (4-ply/weight 1):
32 sts and 44 rounds = 4in (10cm) in stockinette/
stocking st in the round on smaller needles

Light worsted (DK/8-ply/weight 3):
24 sts and 36 rounds = 4in (10cm) in stockinette/
stocking st in the round on smaller needles

Yarn

Fingering (4-ply/weight 1):
YARN A: variegated light gold (Gold Rush)
YARN B: red (Corset)
YARN C: cream (Naked)

Light worsted (DK/8-ply/weight 3):
YARN A: mustard tweed (193 Cumin)
YARN B: dark navy tweed (170 Seafarer)
YARN C: light grey tweed (197 Alabaster)

Needles

Fingering (4-ply/weight 1):
2.25mm (US 1, UK 13) and 2.5mm (US 1.5, UK 12/13)

Light worsted (DK/8-ply/weight 3):
3.25mm (US 3, UK 10) and 3.5mm (US 4, UK 9/10)

Instructions

HAT

Using yarn A and smaller needles, cast on 48 sts. Distribute sts evenly across needles and join for working in the round. Place BOR marker.

Rounds 1-5: k all - 5 rounds.

Round 6: k35, place removable M in WS of first st on left needle st to mark the start for picking up body sts, k to end.

Round 7: (k12, M1L, PM) three times, k12, M1L - 4-st inc (52 sts).

> **NOTE:** in the rounds that follow, BOR marker is a shaping marker.

Round 8: k all.

Join yarn B.

Round 9: using yarn B, k all.

Rounds 10-12: using yarn A, k all - 3 rounds.

Round 13: using yarn A, (k to 2 sts before M, k2tog, SM) four times - 4-st dec (48 sts).

Rounds 14-18: repeat Rounds 9-13 one more time - 5 rounds (44 sts).

Round 19: using yarn B, k all.

Rounds 20 and 21: using yarn A, sl1 wyib, k to end - 2 rounds.

Round 22: using yarn A, sl1 wyib, (k to 2 sts before M, k2tog, SM) four times - 4-st dec (40 sts).

Rounds 23-42: repeat Rounds 19-22 five more times - 20 rounds (20 sts).

Round 43: using yarn B, k all.

Rounds 44-46: using yarn A, sl1 wyib, k to end - 3 rounds.

Round 47: using yarn B, k all.

Rounds 48 and 49: using yarn A, sl1 wyib, k to end - 2 rounds.

Round 50: using yarn A, sl1 wyib, (k to 2 sts before M, k2tog, SM) four times - 4-st dec (16 sts).

Rounds 51-66: repeat Rounds 43-50 two more times - 16 rounds (8 sts).

Round 67: using yarn B and removing M as you go, k all.

Rounds 68-70: using yarn A, sl1 wyib, k to end - 3 rounds.

Round 71: using yarn B, ssk-M, (k2tog) three times - 4-st dec (4 sts).

Place a removable M in one st. Rearrange sts on one needle.

> **TIP:** when working striped I-cord, make sure to bring the working yarn behind the unused yarn.

Rounds 72-74: using yarn A, work I-cord - 3 rounds.

Round 75: using yarn B, work I-cord.

Rounds 76-91: repeat Rounds 72-75 four more times - 16 rounds.

Rounds 92-95 (light worsted/DK/8-ply ONLY): repeat Rounds 72-75 one more time - 4 rounds.

Cut yarn, leaving 6in (15cm) tails. Thread yarn B tail onto a yarn needle then take through the live stitches on the needle from right to left. Bury yarn A down the I-cord and trim. Use the yarn B end to sew the hat as shown opposite, sewing the end of the I-cord to the round in which you placed the removable M at the beginning of the I-cord. Remove this M, but keep the one placed in Round 6. Weave in ends, remembering that the WS of the rolled brim is the stockinette/stocking st side.

Pattern note

The stripes in the hat are frequent enough to carry the yarn up the inside of the hat, but not the body. In the body, tie the ends of yarn A snugly after knitting 2 rounds in yarn B. This will help minimize the jog. Don't bother to trim the tail ends - they will just act as stuffing.

BODY

Fold the brim and about one-third of the hat back. Using smaller needles and working on the WS of the hat, pick up 1 st in every st in Round 6, beginning with the st to the left of the removable M (48 sts). Remove M.

Join to work in the round. Join yarn B and place BOR marker.

Rounds 1-7: using yarn B, k all - 7 rounds.

Round 8: using yarn B, (k16, PM) two times, k16.

> NOTE: in the rounds that follow, BOR marker is a shaping marker.

Round 9: using yarn B, (k2, M1L, k to 2 sts before M, M1R, k2, SM) three times - 6-st inc (54 sts).

Round 10: using yarn B, k all

Join yarn A.

Round 11: using yarn A, k all.

Cut yarn A.

Rounds 12-18: using yarn B, k all - 7 rounds.

Rounds 19-48: repeat Rounds 9-18 three more times - 30 rounds (72 sts).

Rounds 49 and 50: using yarn B, k all - 2 rounds.

Join yarn A.

Round 51: using yarn A, k all.

Cut yarn A.

Rounds 52-58: using yarn B, k all - 7 rounds.

Rounds 59-68: repeat Rounds 49-58 one more time - 10 rounds.

Rounds 69 and 70: using yarn B, k all - 2 rounds.

Cut yarn B. Join yarn A and use it for the remainder of the body.

Round 71: k all.

Round 72: p all.

Round 73: (k12, PM, k12, SM) three times - 6 markers in place.

Weave in the end from the beginning of the body and block gnome.

Stuff hat with fluffy stuffing.

Decrease Round: (k to 2 sts before M, k2tog, SM) six times - 6-st dec.

Repeat Decrease Round until each section has 7 sts (42 sts total).

Stuff body with fluffy stuffing up to the second to last stripe of yarn A.

Repeat Decrease Round until each section has 4 sts (24 sts total).

Stuff the body with weighted stuffing up to the garter ridge. Cover with a very thin layer of stuffing so the pellets don't jump out as you finish.

Repeat Decrease Round until only 6 sts remain, removing M. Cut yarn. Thread tail onto a yarn needle and take through remaining sts, pulling them closed. Weave in the end (see also Pattern Note on page 71).

Pattern note

Gnolan is tall and skinny so test for stability by wiggling him on your palm before sealing up the bottom. If needed, remove some fluffy stuffing from the body and replace with additional weighted stuffing.

BEARD

Leaving a 6in (15cm) tail for attaching later, cast on 15 sts with the long-tail cast-on method, using yarn C and larger needles.

Rows 1-6: sl1 wyib, k to last st, p1 - 6 rows.

Row 7 (RS): sl1 wyib, ssk-M, k to last st, p1 - 1-st dec (14 sts).

Row 8 (WS): sl1 wyib, k to last st, p1.

Rows 9-12: repeat Rows 7 and 8 two more times - 4 rows (12 sts).

Row 13: sl1 wyib, ssk-M, k to last 3 sts, k2tog, p1 - 2-st dec (10 sts).

Rows 14-18: sl1 wyib, k to last st, p1 - 5 rows.

Rows 19-24: repeat Rows 13-18 one more time - 6 rows (8 sts).

Row 25: sl1 wyib, ssk-M, k to last st, p1 - 1-st dec (7 sts).

Rows 26-30: sl1 wyib, k to last st, p1 - 5 rows.

Rows 31-48: repeat Rows 25-30 three more times - 18 rows (4 sts).

Row 49: ssk-M, k2tog and do not turn work - 2-st dec (2 sts).

Rows 50-65: work I-cord - 16 rows.

Cut yarn, thread tail onto a yarn needle then take through sts from right to left.

Sew the end of the I-cord to the beard at the beginning of the I-cord so that it curls up and to the left (opposite the hat swirl). Then stitch the circle to the side of the beard for about 2 garter ridges. Weave in this end, leaving the cast-on end for later. Soak and lay Gnolan flat to dry.

LITTLE FEATURES

Make:

- 2 Large Arms (see page 20) using larger needles and yarns C and B.
- 1 Large Nose (see page 23) using larger needles and yarn C.

MAKING UP

Sew beard onto first round of body, keeping things tidy since the brim is rolled and Gnolan likes his beard to be stylish (he has a hankering to enter the Bracelet Beard category in the World Beard Competition). Centre and sew nose on top of beard. Sew arms onto first round of body at the corners of the beard.

ABOVE, FROM LEFT TO RIGHT: light worsted (DK/8-ply/weight 3) version;
fingering (4-ply/weight 1) version.

Gnicole
THE CABLED GNOME

**Gnicole likes elderberry and hyssop tea in the morning,
and ties feathers in her beard before a disco in the evening.
In between, she maps root systems for the Woodland Council.**

Height

Fingering (4-ply/weight 1):
11in (28cm)

Light worsted (DK/8-ply/weight 3):
14in (35.5cm)

Gauge/tension

Fingering (4-ply/weight 1):
32 sts and 44 rounds = 4in (10cm) in stockinette/
stocking st in the round on smaller needles

Light worsted (DK/8-ply/weight 3):
24 sts and 36 rounds = 4in (10cm) in stockinette/
stocking st in the round on smaller needles

Yarn

Fingering (4-ply/weight 1):
YARN A: gold (Old Gold)
YARN B: teal (Blackwatch)
YARN C: cream (Naked)

Light worsted (DK/8-ply/weight 3):
YARN A: mid-grey tweed (191 Granite)
YARN B: mint green tweed (209 Eden)
YARN C: light grey tweed (197 Alabaster)

Needles

Fingering (4-ply/weight 1):
2.25mm (US 1, UK 13) and 2.5mm (US 1.5, UK 12/13)

Light worsted (DK/8-ply/weight 3):
3.25mm (US 3, UK 10) and 3.5mm (US 4, UK 9/10)

Cable needle

Instructions

HAT

Using yarn A and smaller needles, cast on 60 sts. Distribute sts evenly across needles and join for working in the round. Place BOR marker.

Rounds 1–10: (k3, p3) around - 10 rounds.

Round 11: k all.

Place removable M in first st of Round 11 on WS to mark the start for picking up body sts.

Rounds 12–18: (k3, p3) around - 7 rounds.

Rounds 19–94: either follow Charts 1 and 2 or Written Instructions on pages 81 and 82. Chart 1 applies to Rounds 19–62, and Chart 2 applies to Rounds 63–94.

KEY:

- ☐ k
- ⅄ M1L
- • p
- ⃥ ssk-M
- ⃥ p2tog
- ▱ 3/2 RC
- ▱ 3/3 RC

Written Instructions for Chart 1

Round 19: ((k1, M1L) three times, p3) ten times –
30-st inc (90 sts).

Rounds 20 and 21: (k6, p3) ten times - 2 rounds.

Round 22: (3/3 RC, p3) ten times.

Rounds 23-27: (k6, p3) ten times - 5 rounds.

Rounds 28-33: repeat Rounds 22-27 one more time –
6 rounds.

Round 34: as Round 22.

Rounds 35-38: (k6, p3) ten times - 4 rounds.

Round 39: (ssk-M, k4, p3) ten times – 10-st dec (80 sts).

Round 40: (3/2 RC, p3) ten times.

Rounds 41-45: (k5, p3) ten times - 5 rounds.

Round 46: as Round 40.

Rounds 47-50: (k5, p3) ten times - 4 rounds.

Round 51: (k5, p1, p2tog) ten times – 10-st dec (70 sts).

Round 52: (3/2 RC, p2) ten times.

Rounds 53-57: (k5, p2) ten times - 5 rounds.

Round 58: as Round 52.

Rounds 59-62: (k5, p2) ten times - 4 rounds.

CHART 1

Repeat Chart 1 ten times
per round.

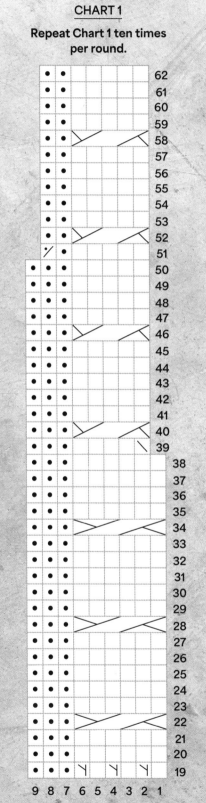

Written Instructions for Chart 2

Round 63: (ssk-M, k3, p2) ten times - 10-st dec (60 sts).

Round 64: (2/2 RC, p2) ten times.

Rounds 65-69: (k4, p2) ten times - 5 rounds.

Round 70: as Round 64.

Rounds 71-73: (k4, p2) ten times - 3 rounds.

Round 74: (ssk-M, k2, p2) ten times - 10-st dec (50 sts).

Round 75: (2/1 RC, p2) ten times.

Rounds 76-78: (k3, p2) ten times - 3 rounds.

Rounds 79-82: repeat Rounds 75-78 one more time - 4 rounds.

Round 83: (2/1 RC, p2tog) ten times - 10-st dec (40 sts).

Rounds 84 and 85: (k3, p1) ten times - 2 rounds.

Round 86: (ssk-M, k1, p1) ten times - 10-st dec (30 sts).

Round 87: (1/1 RC, p1) ten times.

Rounds 88 and 89: (k2, p1) ten times - 2 rounds.

Rounds 90-92: repeat Rounds 87-89 one more time - 3 rounds.

Round 93: (1/1 RC, p1) ten times.

Round 94: (k2, p1) ten times.

KEY:

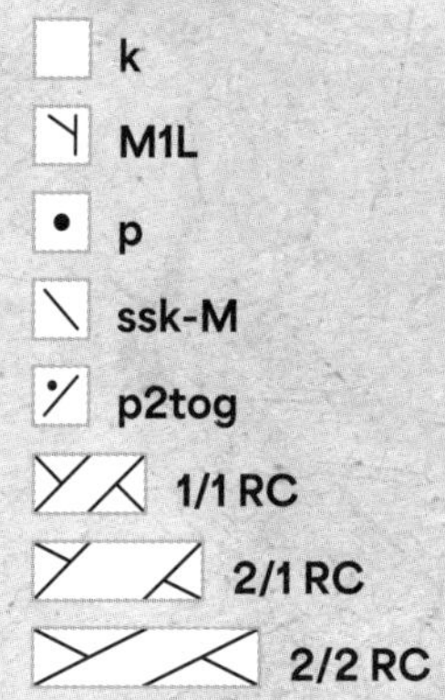

☐	k
⅂	M1L
•	p
\	ssk-M
⟋	p2tog
⤬ (2 st)	1/1 RC
⤬ (3 st)	2/1 RC
⤬ (4 st)	2/2 RC

CHART 2

Repeat Chart 2 ten times per round.

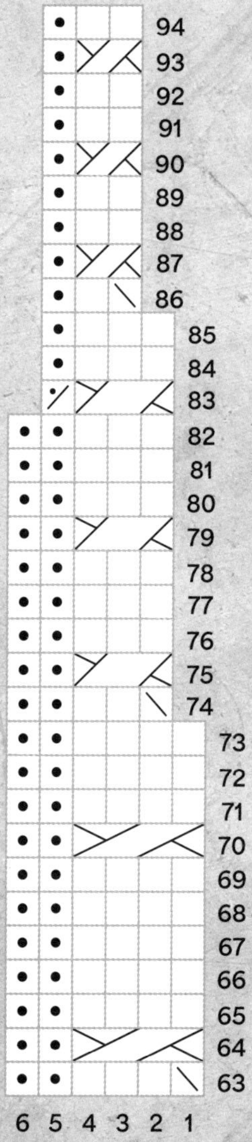

6	5	4	3	2	1	Round
•						94
•	1/1 RC	→				93
•						92
•						91
•	1/1 RC	→				90
•						89
•						88
•	1/1 RC	→				87
•		\				86
•						85
•						84
⟋		2/1 RC	→	→	\	83
•	•					82
•	•					81
•	•					80
•	•		2/1 RC	→	→	79
•	•					78
•	•					77
•	•					76
•	•		2/1 RC	→	→	75
•	•				\	74
•	•					73
•	•					72
•	•					71
•	•	2/2 RC	→	→	→	70
•	•					69
•	•					68
•	•					67
•	•					66
•	•					65
•	•	2/2 RC	→	→	→	64
•	•				\	63

Columns (right to left): 6 5 4 3 2 1

Round 95: (k2tog, p1) nine times, k2tog - 10-st dec. Leave last st unworked. New BOR (20 sts).

Round 96: (k2tog) ten times - 10-st dec (10 sts).

Rounds 97 and 98: k all - 2 rounds.

Round 99: (k2tog) five times - 5-st dec (5 sts).

Cut yarn. Thread yarn onto yarn needle and take through remaining sts. Weave in ends.

ABOVE, FROM LEFT TO RIGHT: Gnicole the Cabled Gnome, light worsted (DK/8-ply/ weight 3) version; Gnectar the Marled Gnome (page 86), light worsted (DK/8-ply/ weight 3) version.

BODY

Fold the brim back. Hold the hat with the point down and the opening facing you. Using smaller needles and working on the WS of the hat, pick up 1 st in every st in Round 11 of the hat (marked by the round of all purls now visible), beginning with the st to the left of the removable M – 60 sts. Use the top half of the sts so the bottom half shows from the front and is a crisp line for the brim (see the bottom photograph on page 15). Remove M.

Join to work in the round. Join yarn B.

Place BOR marker.

Rounds 1–5: k all – 5 rounds.

Round 6: (k20, PM) twice, k20.

> NOTE: in the rounds that follow, BOR marker is a shaping marker.

Round 7: (k2, M1L, k to 2 sts before M, M1R, k2, SM) three times – 6-st inc (66 sts).

Rounds 8–16: k all – 9 rounds.

Rounds 17–36: repeat Rounds 7–16 two more times – 20 rounds (78 sts).

Weave in the end from the beginning of the body.

Block Gnicole, because cables love a chance to settle into their purpose.

Round 37: p all.

Round 38: k13, PM, (k13, SM, k13, PM) twice, k13 – 6 markers in place.

Stuff hat with fluffy stuffing. Her hat is tall and stretchy – avoid the temptation to overstuff. Don't make the hat wider than the body fabric stretches.

Decrease Round: (k to 2 sts before M, k2tog, SM) six times – 6-st dec.

Repeat Decrease Round until each section has 6 sts (36 sts total).

Stuff two-thirds of the body with fluffy stuffing.

Repeat Decrease Round until each section has 4 sts (24 sts total).

Stuff the body with weighted stuffing up to the garter ridge. Cover it with a very thin layer of stuffing so the pellets don't jump out as you finish.

Repeat Decrease Round until only 6 sts remain, removing M.

Cut yarn. Thread tail onto a yarn needle and take through remaining sts, pulling them closed.

Weave in the end.

LITTLE FEATURES

Make:

- 2 Medium Arms (see page 20) using larger needles and yarns C and B.
- 1 Wide and Curly Beard (see page 22) using larger needles and yarn C.
- 1 Large Nose (see page 23) using larger needles and yarn C.
- 1 Tassel (see page 25) with 25 wraps of yarn A. Finished height of tassel: 1¾in (4.5cm) for fingering (4-ply/weight 1) size or 2in (5cm) for light worsted (DK/8-ply/weight 3) size.

MAKING UP

Fold brim up. Sew beard onto first round of body. Note that the top of the beard remains visible, so keep your stitches tidy. Centre and sew nose on top of beard. Sew arms onto first round of body at the corners of the beard. Attach tassel to top of hat. Brim remains folded up.

> NOTE: during assembly Gnicole may get out of shape, so gently roll her on a table to even out the stuffing once she's done.

ABOVE, FROM LEFT TO RIGHT:
fingering (4-ply/weight 1) version;
light worsted (DK/8-ply/weight 3) version.

Gnectar
THE MARLED GNOME

Gnectar's house is nestled in a dell with very good soil. Tall rhubarb plants shade his southern windows in summer, and a thicket of raspberry bushes shield the house from the north winds in winter. If you're ever invited to his house for scones and jam, be sure to accept!

Height

Fingering (4-ply/weight 1):
11¼in (28.5cm)

Light worsted (DK/8-ply/weight 3):
14½in (37cm)

Gauge/tension

Fingering (4-ply/weight 1):
22 sts and 32 rounds = 4in (10cm) in stockinette/
stocking st in the round on smaller needles

Light worsted (DK/8-ply/weight 3):
18 sts and 26 rounds = 4in (10cm) in stockinette/
stocking st in the round on smaller needles

Yarn

Fingering (4-ply/weight 1):
YARN A: variegated light gold (Gold Rush)
YARN B: red (Corset)
YARN C: gold (Old Gold)
YARN D: cream (Naked)
YARN E: teal (Blackwatch)

Light worsted (DK/8-ply/weight 3):
YARN A: mustard tweed (193 Cumin)
YARN B: mint green tweed (209 Eden)
YARN C: mid-grey tweed (191 Granite)
YARN D: light grey tweed (197 Alabaster)
YARN E: dark navy tweed (170 Seafarer)

Needles

Fingering (4-ply/weight 1):
3.25mm (US 3, UK 10) and 3.5mm (US 4, UK 9/10)

Light worsted (DK/8-ply/weight 3):
4mm (US 6, UK 8) and 4.5mm (US 7, UK 7)

Pattern notes

- Except for the beard, Gnectar is knitted with two strands of yarn.

- If you're playing with your own colours, experiment by holding the sets of two colours together and wrapping them around a ruler, before committing them to your needles.

- A not-so-hidden ninth gnome can be made with this pattern! For each weight, use just one strand of yarn rather than two, and the needles and the gauge/tension of the relevant weight gnome from another pattern in this book.

Instructions

HAT

Using yarns A and B held together and smaller needles, cast on 36 sts. Distribute sts evenly across needles and join for working in the round. Place BOR marker.

Rounds 1-7: k all – 7 rounds.

Place removable M in first st of Round 7 on WS to mark the start for picking up body sts.

Round 8: (k9, M1L, PM) four times – 4-st inc (40 sts).

> NOTE: in the rounds that follow, BOR marker is a shaping marker.

Rounds 9-13: k all – 5 rounds.

Round 14: (k to 2 sts before M, k2tog, SM) four times – 4-st dec (36 sts).

Rounds 15-18: k all – 4 rounds.

Cut yarn B and join yarn C.

Rounds 19-33: using yarns A and C, repeat Rounds 14-18 three more times – 15 rounds (24 sts).

Cut yarn C and join yarn D.

Rounds 34-58: using yarns A and D, repeat Rounds 14-18 five more times – 25 rounds (4 sts).

Round 59: removing M as you go, k2tog, k2 – 1-st dec (3 sts).

I-Cord Toppers:

Start with st 1, setting aside sts 2 and 3 on st holders or waste yarn.

Round 1: kfb – 1-st inc (2 sts).

Rounds 2-16: work I-cord – 15 rounds.

Cut yarns, thread tails on a yarn needle and take them through the live stitches, from right to left. Bury yarn ends down the I-cord and trim. Tie I-cord in a knot.

Repeat with st 2, rejoining yarns to work I-cord.

Repeat with st 3, leaving 6in (15cm) tails of both yarns when you join. Once you've worked the I-cord, tightly wrap these ends around the tip of the hat three times to help the I-cords stand, then weave in all ends, remembering that the WS of the rolled brim is the stockinette/stocking st side.

BODY

Fold the brim and about one-third of the hat back. Using smaller needles and working on the WS of the hat, pick up 1 st in every st in Round 7, beginning with the st to the left of the removable M (36 sts). Remove M.

Join to work in the round. Join yarns B and E and place BOR marker.

Round 1: k all.

Round 2: k4, (PM, k9) three times, PM, k5.

> NOTE: in the rounds that follow, BOR marker is NOT a shaping marker.

Round 3: (k to 1 st before M, M1R, k1, SM, k1, M1L) four times, k to end – 8-st inc (44 sts).

Rounds 4 and 5: k all – 2 rounds.

Rounds 6-14: repeat Rounds 3-5 three more times – 9 rounds (68 sts).

Rounds 15-38: k all – 24 rounds.

Round 39: (k to 3 sts before M, ssk-M, k1, SM, k1, k2tog) four times, k to end – 8-st dec (60 sts).

Round 40: k all.

Weave in the ends from the beginning of the body. Stuff the hat with fluffy stuffing.

Rounds 41-48: repeat Rounds 39 and 40 four more times – 8 rounds (28 sts).

Firmly stuff the body with fluffy stuffing up to about the start of the decreases.

Round 49: removing M as you go, (k2, k2tog) seven times – 7-st dec (21 sts).

Round 50: k2tog, k to end – 1-st dec (20 sts).

Round 51: k all.

Fill with weighted stuffing. Cover with a very thin layer of stuffing so the pellets don't jump out as you finish.

Round 52: (k2tog) ten times – 10-st dec (10 sts).

Round 53: (k2tog) five times – 5-st dec (5 sts).

Cut yarn. Thread tail onto a yarn needle and take through remaining sts, pulling them closed.

Weave in the end.

LITTLE FEATURES

Make:

- 2 Medium Arms (see page 20) using larger needles. Use yarn D held double for the hand, and yarns B and E for the arms.
- 1 Large Nose (see page 23) using larger needles and yarn D held double.
- 1 Garter-stitch Beard (see page 22) using smaller needles and only one strand of yarn D.
- 1 Pocket (see page 24) using larger needles and yarns B and C.

MAKING UP

Sew beard onto first round of body, keeping things tidy since the brim is rolled and won't cover the beard (and Gnectar likes his beard to look stylish). Centre and sew nose on the top edge of the beard. Sew arms onto first round of body at the corners of the beard.

Sew pocket onto body as shown, leaving the widest edge open. Align the top inside corner under the corner of the beard and bottom corner about 5 rounds lower. (Before sewing, test that the hands can reach inside the pockets.)

OPPOSITE, FROM LEFT TO RIGHT:
light worsted (DK/8-ply/weight 3) version;
fingering (4-ply/weight 1) version.

Charts of Everything

GNOME	Height	Needles used	Colours used (from Miss Babs Katahdin 437)	Grams needed (+ 15% buffer)
Gnoodles (page 28)	4½in (11.5cm)	2.25mm (US 1, UK 13) and 2.5mm (US 1.5, UK 12/13)	Yarn A: Old Gold Yarn B: Corset Yarn C: Naked	Yarn A: 5g Yarn B: 8g Yarn C: 3g
Gnoddy (page 34)	5½in (14cm)	2.25mm (US 1, UK 13) and 2.5mm (US 1.5, UK 12/13)	Yarn A: Old Gold Yarn B: Gold Rush Yarn C: Naked Yarn D: Blackwatch	Yarn A: 3g Yarn B: 5g Yarn C:4g Yarn D: 9g
Gnarley† (page 42)	7in (18cm)	2.25mm (US 1, UK 13) and 2.5mm (US 1.5, UK 12/13)	Yarn A: Old Gold Yarn B: Naked	Yarn A: 20g Yarn B: 4g
Gnatalia† (page 52)	7½in (19cm)	2.25mm (US 1, UK 13) and 2.5mm (US 1.5, UK 12/13)	Yarn A: Blackwatch Yarn B: Corset Yarn C: Naked Yarn D: Old Gold Yarn E: Carina	Yarn A: 4g Yarn B: 3g Yarn C: 17g Yarn D: 3g Yarn E: 18g
Gnorri† (page 62)	8in (20cm)	2.25mm (US 1, UK 13) and 2.5mm (US 1.5, UK 12/13)	Yarn A: Corset Yarn B: Carina Yarn C: Naked	Yarn A: 12g Yarn B: 15g Yarn C: 5g
Gnolan† (page 68)	10in (25.5cm)	2.25mm (US 1, UK 13) and 2.5mm (US 1.5, UK 12/13)	Yarn A: Gold Rush Yarn B: Corset Yarn C: Naked	Yarn A: 14g Yarn B: 21g Yarn C: 5g
Gnicole (page 78)	11in (28cm)	2.25mm (US 1, UK 13) and 2.5mm (US 1.5, UK 12/13)	Yarn A: Old Gold Yarn B: Blackwatch Yarn C: Naked	Yarn A: 26g Yarn B: 15g Yarn C: 5g
Gnectar (page 86)	11¼in (28.5cm)	3.25mm (US 3, UK 10) and 3.5mm (US 4, UK 9/10)	Yarn A: Gold Rush Yarn B: Corset Yarn C: Old Gold Yarn D: Naked Yarn E: Blackwatch	Yarn A: 10g Yarn B: 29g Yarn C: 5g Yarn D: 10g Yarn E: 21g

LIGHT WORSTED (DK/8-PLY/WEIGHT 3) SIZE

GNOME	Height	Needles used	Colours used (from Rowan Felted Tweed)	Grams needed (+ 15% buffer)
Gnoodles (page 28)	6in (15cm)	3.25mm (US 3, UK 10) and 3.5mm (US 4, UK 9/10)	Yarn A: 170 Seafarer Yarn B: 191 Granite Yarn C: 197 Alabaster	Yarn A: 5g Yarn B: 7g Yarn C: 3g
Gnoddy (page 34)	7¼in (18.5cm)	3.25mm (US 3, UK 10) and 3.5mm (US 4, UK 9/10)	Yarn A: 196 Barn Red Yarn B: 170 Seafarer Yarn C: 197 Alabaster Yarn D: 193 Cumin	Yarn A: 10g Yarn B: 6g Yarn C: 3g Yarn D: 11g
Gnarley† (page 42)	9in (23cm)	3.25mm (US 3, UK 10) and 3.5mm (US 4, UK 9/10)	Yarn A: 196 Barn Red Yarn B: 197 Alabaster	Yarn A: 30g Yarn B: 5g
Gnatalia† (page 52)	9½in (24cm)	3.25mm (US 3, UK 10) and 3.5mm (US 4, UK 9/10)	Yarn A: 196 Barn Red Yarn B: 170 Seafarer Yarn C: 197 Alabaster Yarn D: 209 Eden Yarn E: 193 Cumin	Yarn A: 5g Yarn B: 4g Yarn C: 17g Yarn D: 4g Yarn E: 24g
Gnorri† (page 62)	10½in (26.5cm)	3.25mm (US 3, UK 10) and 3.5mm (US 4, UK 9/10)	Yarn A: 209 Eden Yarn B: 196 Barn Red Yarn C: 197 Alabaster	Yarn A: 11g Yarn B: 19g Yarn C: 5g
Gnolan† (page 68)	13½in (34.5cm)	3.25mm (US 3, UK 10) and 3.5mm (US 4, UK 9/10)	Yarn A: 193 Cumin Yarn B: 170 Seafarer Yarn C: 197 Alabaster	Yarn A: 16g Yarn B: 22g Yarn C: 6g
Gnicole (page 78)	14in (35.5cm)	3.25mm (US 3, UK 10) and 3.5mm (US 4, UK 9/10)	Yarn A: 191 Granite Yarn B: 209 Eden Yarn C: 197 Alabaster	Yarn A: 38g Yarn B: 20g Yarn C: 5g
Gnectar (page 86)	14½in (37cm)	4mm (US 6, UK 8) and 4.5mm (US 7, UK 7)	Yarn A: 193 Cumin Yarn B: 209 Eden Yarn C: 191 Granite Yarn D: 197 Alabaster Yarn E: 170 Seafarer	Yarn A: 13g Yarn B: 30g Yarn C: 6g Yarn D: 12g Yarn E: 25g

† NOTE: Since the brim stitch count is the same, you can mix and match the different hat styles with the different body shapes for Gnorri, Gnatalia, Gnolan and Gnarley.

Thunderous Applause

To my family, who inspire me to be bold and teach me to put important things first.

To my parents, for being great people who showed me how to walk unconventional paths with an open heart. And Dad, thanks for all the help with photography.

To my design buddies, Lisa Ross, Mary Hull, and Jesie Ostermiller; your ideas, creativity and honesty are vital.

To my test knitters, for donating their time to make certain these knitting patterns make sense: smoodog/Jean Cain, maryeb, staubkoernchen/Anneli, Jaime Louise Miller, JeepGeek/ Tara P, MollyHatChick, RevJan, wendebular/Wendy, Laura Gorton, Mamacelebrates/Lise, Deb Smith, mwachen/Melanie, Joseybug.

To the thousands of knitters who have responded with such joyous enthusiasm to my gnome patterns; your energy helped create the Grimblewoods.

And to Emily Adam, my editor, who fulfilled my childhood dreams and asked me to be an author.

First published in 2024

Search Press Limited
Wellwood, North Farm Road,
Tunbridge Wells, Kent TN2 3DR

Book ISBN: 978-1-80092-202-0
ebook ISBN: 978-1-80093-186-2

Suppliers
If you have difficulty in obtaining any of the materials and equipment mentioned
in this book, then please visit the Search Press website for details of suppliers:
www.searchpress.com

Bookmarked
For further ideas and inspiration, and to join our free online community,
visit www.bookmarkedhub.com

Further inspiration
visit www.imaginedlandscapes.com
YouTube channel via @imaginedlandscapes
Instagram via @imagined_landscapes
Podcast via www.imaginedlandscapes.com/podcast/
Ravelry via www.ravelry.com/groups/imagined-landscapes

MIX
Paper | Supporting
responsible forestry
FSC® C016973

FSC
www.fsc.org